WHEN PREPARATION MEETS OPPORTUNITY

GERALD D. IRONS, SR. AND MYRNA J. IRONS

Copyright © 2014
by GERALD D. IRONS, SR. AND MYRNA J. IRONS

WHEN PREPARATION MEETS OPPORTUNITY
by GERALD D. IRONS, SR. AND MYRNA J. IRONS

Printed in the United States of America

ISBN 9781628716351

All rights reserved solely by the authors. The authors guarantee all contents are original and do not infringe upon the legal rights of any other person or work. No part of this book may be reproduced in any form without the permission of the author. The views expressed in this book are not necessarily those of the publisher.

www.xulonpress.com

Table Of Contents

Foreword vii

Introduction xiii

Dedication xix

Chapter 1: My Heroes 21

Chapter 2: My Bedroom, the Hallway 25

Chapter 3: What is a Scholarship? 27

Chapter 4: A Clock-Watcher 31

Chapter 5: I Was Not College Material..... 33

Chapter 6: Scholarship! We Only Won
One Football Game 38

Chapter 7: Always Do Your Best 41

Chapter 8: The Immaculate Reception 45

Chapter 9: Johnny Carson – The Tonight Show 50

Chapter 10: The University of Chicago, MBA 52

Chapter 11: Law School and the Cleveland Browns 55

Chapter 12: Retiring from the NFL – Service Above Self 61

Chapter 13: Prepare Yourself for the Super Bowls of Your Life 68

Chapter 14: Gerald D. Irons, Sr. Junior High School 91

Chapter 15: Keys To Success 97

Chapter 16: My Poems 103

Chapter 17: Poems from a NFL Linebacker 105

Foreword

My introduction to Gerald Irons was during the 1970–1971 season with the Oakland Raiders professional football team. The Raiders were a team known for toughness and the "will to win." Pro Bowlers and eventual Hall Of Fame coaches and players included owner Al Davis, head coach John Madden and players Art Shell, Willie Brown, Cliff Branch, Otis Sistrunk, George Blanda, Jim Otto, Gene Upshaw, Fred Biletnikoff, Daryle Lamonica, Bob Brown, Ken Stabler, Raymond Chester, Jack Tatum, Gus Otto, George Atkinson, Bubba Smith, Marv Hubbard, Phil Villapiano, Morris Bradshaw, Ben Davidson, Bill Laskey, Duane Benson, Dan Connors,

Charlie Smith, Mike Siani, Clarence Davis, Tony Cline, Ray Guy, Horace Jones, Nemiah Wilson, Tom Keating, Rod Sherman, Ron Mix, Bob Moore, Carleton Oats, Art Thoms, Pete Banaszak, Ira Matthews, Eldridge Dickey, Monte Johnson and Dave Casper, to name a few. This was an amazing environment, in which a young man fresh out of college would find himself or get lost in the competitive professional world that is professional football. Gerald and I were assigned to share the same room in rookie training camp and became roommates. We were also vying for positions, at outside linebacker, on the famed Oakland Raiders defense.

One would think the tendency, when competing for the same job, is to find a way to get rid of the other guy. Instead, football creates a climate where the ultimate competition is with one's self. The fight to strengthen, improve, overcome, persevere and, ultimately, to dominate has much more to do with self than with the opponent or adversary. For anyone who's ever played the game, on a professional level, the added pressure of the "business of football" means talent is not enough. One must also fit into the team concept. Tightly knit players can lead to tightly knit teams. This leads me back to Gerald, or Gerry as I remember calling his name from that first introduction. As roommates, Gerry and I competed but we also cheered each other on. Although he was drafted in the third round, which was quite impressive, and I was undrafted, I always felt that he was rooting for my success.

Gerry was a true team player. He was also a guy I held as a model. Physically gifted, smart and focused were only a few of the traits that were admirable of him. Gerry was also committed to improving not only as a pro football player, but as a human being, as a man of principles. He's a testament to the notion that ability is important, and what you do with that ability and how you do it will determine your true success.

I remember another name ascribe to Gerry. It was "Scrap," as in Scrap Iron, playing on Gerry's last name. That nickname stuck. Still today, guys we played with refer to my friend, Gerry, as "Scrap Iron." What it denotes is a sign of respect, because Gerry was also tough in the trenches. Yet, all evidence shows that his toughness was tempered with a deep faith, generous nature and compassion for all.

I was so honored to had been asked by my friend, and an outstanding human being, husband, father and grandfather, to write this Foreword. The content of this book you're about to read says more about Gerald "Gerry," "Scrap" Irons, as a man of character, throughout the story of his life and the road he's traveled until now. While filled with so much vitality, I'm sure there's a lot of road ahead for him. I'm grateful to be able to say I was there beside Gerry during part of his journey.

We all have our story, but some stories are truly inspirational. The Gerald Irons story is one of them.

Carl Weathers

Carl Weathers is an actor, as well as a former professional football player with the Oakland Raiders. He is well known for playing Apollo Creed in the *Rocky* series of films. He played Dillon in *Predator*, Chubbs Peterson in *Happy Gilmore* and Little Nicky in the television series *Arrested Development*. He also played Hampton Forbes in *The Heat of the Night*. He starred in movies *Force 10 From Navarone*, *Hurricane Smith* and *Action Jackson*.

Carl and I are lifelong friends. He is tremendously gifted and a class act. I will always call him my brother.

Introduction

Gerald Irons was born in Gary, Indiana and is the youngest of seven. He graduated from the University of Maryland – Eastern Shore where he was student government vice president, captain of the football team, named to the Hawks Football Hall of Fame and a member of the Fellowship of Christian Athletes. He earned his Bachelor of Science degree in four years, majoring in Business Administration.

He played linebacker for ten years in the National Football League (NFL), six years with the Oakland Raiders and four years with the Cleveland Browns. During every off-season with the Raiders, he attended The University of Chicago Graduate School of Business and earned his Master's Degree in Business Administration (MBA). After being traded to the Cleveland Browns, he attended the John Marshall Law School, after practicing football during the day. He hosted the "PM Magazine Show" on television and the "Gerald Irons Sports Report" on radio. He was voted Team Captain by his teammates and received several Golden Helmet Awards. Gerald was named an "Oakland Raiders Legend" and is listed among the "100 Greatest Cleveland Browns" of all time. He was inducted into The Indiana Football Hall of Fame.

During his four years in Cleveland, he was named "Man of the Year" by the Cleveland Jaycees and served as a National Television Spokesman for United Way. He was invited to The White House by President Jimmy Carter to discuss solutions to youth unemployment in America. He served as a Liaison for U.S. Senator John Glenn's re-election. In Gary,

Indiana, he received the "Outstanding Garyite Award" from Mayor Richard Hatcher and a day was named in his honor. He was named one of the "Ten Outstanding People in the World" by the Osaka Junior Chamber of Commerce in Osaka, Japan. The Mayor of Osaka presented Gerald with a "Gold Key" to the city. He spent a month in Japan, representing the United States of America at the "Ten Outstanding Young Persons Conference." While in Japan, he met with the Emperor, the Prime Minister, the Crown Prince and Crown Princess. He also speaks the Japanese language.

He was Vice President of Business Development thirty-two years with The Woodlands Development Company, a Howard Hughes Company, located in The Woodlands, Texas. He was also Vice President of Colliers International. He is a Texas commercial real estate broker. He gives productivity improvement presentations to companies and universities, such as ExxonMobil, Norfolk

Southern Railroad, Shell Oil, Dow Chemical, AT&T, Smith & Nephew, Abbott Laboratories, Peter Burwash International, Southern Pacific Railroad, Rice University, Georgetown University and Lone Star College, among others. He is also a graduate of the Houston FBI Citizens Academy.

Gerald retired from the Conroe Independent School District Board of Trustees after serving twenty-two years. The CISD School Board named a new school, the Gerald D. Irons Sr. Junior High School, after him. He is the first and only NFL player to have a school named in his honor.

Gerald and his wife Myrna were high school sweethearts in Gary, Indiana and have been married forty-four wonderful years. They have three sons, all played football at Division I universities on full scholarships. Gerald Jr. graduated from the University of Nebraska, Jarrett graduated from the University of Michigan (two-time team captain) and Grant graduated from the University of Notre Dame (two-time team captain). They have one grandson, Gerald Irons III, who was named "Student of the Year" and "Unsung Hero" in CISD. All five members of the Irons family were honored as "Original Hometown Heroes," selected by The Woodlands residents.

Gerald is an Elder at Impact Church in The Woodlands. He and Myrna are founding members.

Dedication and Acknowledgments

We dedicate this book to our family and friends, who have always encouraged and supported us.

Special acknowledgments to our parents; Earmon and Sycbrathia Irons, Lester and Venita Wise, our sons; Gerald Jr., Jarrett, Grant and grandson, Gerald III.

Gerald's sisters and brothers; Henry, Eula, Earmon, Lethenius, Syrathia and Evie. Myrna's brother and sister; DeWayne and Leslie.

All of you inspire us daily to be the best.

We give God all of the glory.
We love you.

Gerald and Myrna

Chapter One

My Heroes

My heroes were my mother and father. They had an eighth-grade education; the two of them were the smartest people I have ever known. My parents valued education. They were a hardworking and devoted couple. They were faithful to their church, and often people would stop by and ask for prayer. My parents would invite them into our home, feed them and pray for them. One of our neighbors told me that our home had more prayer inside of it than some churches.

My parents knew how difficult life would be without a good education. They encouraged all seven of their children to work hard in school and go to college. All seven graduated from college. One of their legacies is their grandchildren have graduated from college also.

I was fourteen pounds at birth, born in my parent's bedroom, and I was their youngest child, the baby. The doctor gave my parents his portable scales, as a memento. As a toddler, I did not want to walk. I only wanted my eldest sister to carry me and she would, with my feet dangling below her knees.

My parents worked in the steel mill to give their children the opportunity to go to college.

When it was time for my parents to go to work, they had me sit on the upstairs steps and look out the window to wait for my brothers and sisters to come home from school. On those steps is where I learned to wait, dream, think and pray. I did this until I was old enough to start school.

GERALD'S FATHER

When Preparation Meets Opportunity

GERALD'S MOTHER

GERALD'S MOTHER AND FATHER

Chapter Two
My Bedroom, The Hallway

With seven children in our home, there was not enough room for me to have a bedroom. The hallway became my bedroom; I loved my bedroom! It was the hallway outside of my parents' and sisters' bedrooms. I decorated the walls with pictures and posters. I slept on a fold-away bed that I stored in the closet each morning. I was proud of my bedroom. Even though it was the hallway, it was my bedroom.

One Saturday morning, while lying in my fold-away bed, I overheard my parents talking about how my father would have to work past retirement age in order to pay for me to go to college. I heard him say to my mother, "We won't have enough money to send Gerald to college, unless I keep working." When I heard this, all I could think about was my father continuing to work double shifts, in that hot steel mill, to pay for my college tuition. My father was aging, yet he would keep working for me to go to college. I was so still on my foldaway bed; I did not move an inch. I didn't want them to know I was listening. I understood the sacrifice and hard work my parents had put in for us to have the opportunity to go to college. I was the youngest of seven children; of two parents who poured out their blood and sweat in the steel mill, who committed themselves to make certain every one of their children attended college. At this time, I was starting the eleventh grade.

Chapter Three
What is a Scholarship?

My heart was heavy after overhearing my parents talking about my father working past retirement age. I did not want him to have to do this, but I did not have an answer to solve this dilemma. I knew I had to find a way. I prayed about this situation.

A week later, college coaches came to my high school football practice to recruit football players. They told my coaches they were looking for players to give them scholarships. After practice, I asked my coach, "What is a scholarship?" My coach said that's when colleges pay for all of your expenses. I was amazed and said, "They will pay for all of my college expenses? My parents would not have to pay for my college tuition? Where do I sign and what do I have to do?" My coach told me that I would have to be an outstanding player, have a good work ethic, be quick, fast, strong, have great conduct and, most importantly, have good grades. This was a prayer answered. However, my grades were terrible and my conduct was horrible.

The next memory that came to mind was when I was in the seventh grade, and my teacher asked the class to stand and tell what we wanted to be when we grew up. Everyone before me said they wanted to be a teacher, doctor, lawyer, etc. When it was my turn, I proudly said, "I want to be a professional football player, businessman, lawyer, get married and be a father."

The teacher said, "Gerald, just choose one; it is humanly impossible to do all of those things. It would take five lifetimes to do all of that. You are the biggest one in the class. Choose football and sit down."

The class laughed at me. I was devastated and embarrassed; even though I was the biggest in the class, I felt small.

When I got home, my parents noticed something was wrong. They asked me, and I told them what happened in class. They shared these words of wisdom with me. "Never let anyone tell you what you cannot do. You control your own destiny; aim high, work hard, never quit and pray." After their talk, I immediately felt better. They believed in me!

When Preparation Meets Opportunity

GERALD IN ROOSEVELT HIGH SCHOOL HALLWAY

Chapter Four
A Clock-Watcher

I was a clock-watcher in school. I would sit in my class, but instead of listening to the teacher, I would watch the minutes jump on the clock; waiting for the bell to ring so I could go to lunch or hang out with my friends. One day, my teacher called me to his desk and told me that he noticed I always watched the clock, instead of paying attention to what he was teaching. He said, "Time will pass, but will you?" That was an impactful statement for me. It reminded me that we all have the same twenty-four hours in a day; but, it's how we use our time that makes all the difference.

I was not using my time wisely, and I knew that somehow I had to make a change to improve my behavior.

GERALD IN GRADE SCHOOL

Chapter Five
I Was Not College Material

Three events happened in my junior year of high school that made me take stock of my actions and myself.

I met a pretty young lady named Myrna Wise, and I felt like I was struck by a thunderbolt. She was very shy. I followed her all over school; when she left her classes, I was there to walk her to her next class. She was a transfer student from our local Catholic high school; she was special and different. Whenever an adult would enter into her classroom, she automatically stood as a sign of respect. After a while, she learned we did not do that. All of the guys wanted to talk to her. She didn't talk to any of us. I had to get rid of my competition right away. I told my teammates and friends not to talk to her; I would help her make her transition to this new school. When I told them this, my fists were balled up. I told them I was going to marry her. I do not know where this thought came from; I just knew that God had brought her into my life.

When her family and friends asked how she liked the new school, she told them the young ladies were friendly but the young men were not friendly; they would not talk to her. She slowly began to talk to me, but she had heard about my reputation of not always having good conduct. I was even expelled from school a few times. She told me I could not come to her home to meet her parents, unless my conduct and grades improved. I was also riding a motorcycle. I fit the bad-boy image entirely.

My mother had to come to school to talk to the principal about expelling me again. I saw my mother crying as I listened to her, trying to convince the principal to let me stay in school. I felt chills; I knew I had let her down. I was crying and I vowed to myself, and to her, that she would never have to come to school again to get me out of trouble. I told her if she ever had to cry for me again, they would only be happy tears. From that day on, she only cried happy tears whenever I was concerned.

I had a scheduled meeting with my guidance counselor to talk about my future. I was expecting her to show me college brochures. Instead, she told me I was not college material. I told her all my brothers and sisters had graduated or were still in college. My parents expected no less from me. She told me for the past two years, I had not prepared myself to go to college. My grades were D's and F's; one teacher even gave me an F+. She handed me some brochures for trade schools and told me this was my future. My immediate thought was I have to go to college, and why did I play around for two years? My parents would be disappointed when they found out.

I told my now-girlfriend, Myrna, what happened in my meeting with the guidance counselor. She told me it was not too late and she would help me study. I had two years to turn my grades around. She taught me how to study, and we began studying together. My grades and conduct improved tremendously. We have been married forty-four wonderful years, and I love her now more than ever. She is everything to me.

I had to make some immediate changes in my life. I needed to take an assessment of myself because I knew better. My parents did not raise me this way. My mission was to get a college scholarship, and honor my parents for all of their hard work and devotion to me. I knew I had to prepare for my opportunity. I learned it is not where you start, but where you finish. I learned it wasn't easy preparing yourself for your future, but you have to. You have to, as Nike says, "Just Do It." One of my favorite sayings is, "You do what you have to do. . . .until you can do what you want to do."

GERALD AND MYRNA AT HIGH SCHOOL PROM

Chapter Six
Scholarship! We Only Won One Football Game

At the end of my junior year, I was well on my way to earning a scholarship.

I worked hard, because I knew there would be college scouts at our games looking to offer scholarships. During my senior year, I tried to make every tackle on both sides of the football field. On offense, I tried to make every block. I was determined to impress the college scouts.

I was lifting weights, working on my speed and quickness, perfecting my tackling techniques and improving my grades and my conduct. I was well on my way to earning a full scholarship. I played on offense, defense and special teams. I was voted Team Captain. I was preparing myself to earn a scholarship.

However, at the end of my senior season, our team only won one game. There were no college scouts calling our coaches to offer football scholarships. I learned that when your team has a losing season, college scouts are not looking to give scholarships. They were not knocking on my door. I was so disappointed; I could not believe what was happening to me. I did everything right, on and off the football field. I realized my father was going to have to work beyond his retirement age in order to pay for me to go to college. I did everything I knew to do. I worked hard in the weight room getting stronger, improved my speed, made a lot of tackles, improved my conduct to exemplary and brought my grades up to A's and B's. Yet, I still did not have a football scholarship. What was I going to do now? All

I could do was what my parents taught me to do, pray.

GERALD'S HIGH SCHOOL SENIOR PICTURE

Chapter Seven
Always Do Your Best

Summer was starting, and I had graduated from high school. I still had not been offered a football scholarship. I finally told my parents what I was trying to do. They asked me, "What is a scholarship?" I explained it to them, but it did not look like I was going to get one. My father told me to not worry about it because he was not sending me to college to play football. He said he was sending me to college to get an education. I still continued to pray about it. I told my father I wanted to play football. My father was firm in his thinking, because he did not want me to get hurt. My mother told my father, "Let him play football, because he loves it and he is good at it. He can play football, get a good education, and we will pray that he won't get hurt." I played over twenty years of contact football in junior high, high school, college and the NFL, and I never had an injury or any surgery.

One evening, I received a telephone call from a high school coach that I had played against. He asked me was I going to college. I told him I was going, but I did not have a football scholarship. He said, "You do now!" He told me he was attending graduate school with a coach who just accepted a college head football-coaching job. He was looking for hard-nose football players and asked if he knew any players that fit that bill. The coach told him he did not have any players like that on his team, but he played against a player that did and had it all. He recommended me. He told him we beat them on the scoreboard, but this guy was all over the field and almost beat us single-handedly. He told me the coach said to call and offer me a full scholarship. As tears were running down my face, I realized that this coach had never seen me play, seen any of my game film or timed me in the 40-yard dash. Yet, he offered me a full college football scholarship. My father could retire; my prayers had been answered.

When Preparation Meets Opportunity

GERALD IN CAP AND GOWN

Chapter Eight
The Immaculate Reception

I went to college, majored in Business Administration, made the Dean's List, played football, was voted Team Captain and named to the University of Maryland E.S. Hawks Hall of Fame. Before I graduated from college, I was drafted, in the third round, by the Oakland Raiders professional football team.

Every year, the Oakland Raiders were in the NFL Playoffs. During one of the playoff games, the Oakland Raiders vs. the Pittsburgh Steelers, I was on the field during the most infamous and controversial play in NFL history called "The Immaculate Reception." A play that has lived a life of its own; this game is still talked about because the officials' call was not legal. The NFL rule at that time, according to Art McNally, NFL Supervisor of Officials, said Rule Seven, Section Five, Article Two, Item One states, "The first player to touch the pass, he, only, continues to be eligible to advance the ball." That was a Pittsburgh Steeler. As soon as the second Pittsburgh Steeler touched the ball, it became an incomplete pass. Therefore, the touchdown ruling was incorrect. The players from both teams were standing around, waiting for the officials to make their call. The Raiders were waiting for the call to be an illegal play, and the Steelers were waiting for the call to be a touchdown. There were thousands of Steeler fans that had rushed onto the field, waiting also for the officials' call. The Steeler fans were going wild and celebrating on the field.

While the Raider players were standing near the officials, we heard the officials call up to the press box and ask for additional security before they announced their call. They were told they did not have extra security. The officials looked at each other, and both raised their arms and signaled "Touchdown!" The NFL has since changed the rule that two offensive players can touch the ball. That play ended my Super Bowl dreams as a Raider. Al Davis always said,

"Once a Raider. . .always a Raider!"

When Preparation Meets Opportunity

GERALD'S OAKLAND RAIDER FOOTBALL PICTURE

The Immaculate Reception

**GERALD'S UNIVERSITY OF MARYLAND, E.S.
GRADUATION WITH HIS PARENTS**

Chapter Nine
Johnny Carson - The Tonight Show

The Miami Dolphins had an undefeated season with a record of 17-0. Their next game was against the Oakland Raiders. If they beat the Raiders, they would set a record for all-time consecutive wins by a NFL team. Two of their players were scheduled to appear on the Tonight Show, the night after the game. The Raiders beat the Dolphins and kept them from getting the record. When the Dolphin players showed up for the Tonight Show, Johnny Carson asked, "I thought we were going to celebrate a victory; I thought you were going to beat the Raiders. What happen?" Both of the players said, "A guy named Gerald Irons happened; you would have thought we said something derogatory about his mother when we touched the ball. He was in our faces, hitting us every time we turned around. He turned us every which way but loose." The NFL named me Defensive Player of the Week.

Chapter Ten

The University of Chicago – MBA

I attended The University of Chicago Graduate School of Business during the off-seasons while playing with the Oakland Raiders. This was quite difficult because the Raiders were in the playoffs every year. After every season, I immediately registered for the new school year. My mission was to earn a Master's of Business Administration (MBA) degree. I had a commitment to excellence, on and off the field.

The school allowed students to take a maximum of three classes per semester. In order to graduate, I needed to take four classes in my last semester. I met with the dean of the business school to get special permission to take the extra course load. He tried to talk me out of it, saying he thought it was too difficult to do, but he approved my request. However, when I went to register for the four classes, two of the classes were taught on the same day and at the same time. The dean told me it was impossible to take two classes that are taught at the same time. I knew that if I prayed, God would show me a way I could take both classes at the same time and complete all four classes to graduate.

I bought two tape recorders. I split time between both classes. During my recess break, I would change classes. I took copious notes, as well as recorded the lectures I missed. I was able to study my notes I took from each class and listen to the recordings. I passed all four classes with great grades and graduated with my MBA. Although the dean advised me not to do it, he told me it had never been done before. He said no student had ever asked him to take two classes that were scheduled at the same time on the same day. I knew God would show me how to accomplish this goal.

Chapter Eleven

Law School and the Cleveland Browns

I was taking my last final examination at the University of Chicago, only one week before graduation. I got an emergency phone call from my wife, informing me that we had been traded. I asked her what team and she said the Cleveland Browns. I said the Browns only won a few games last year; I can help them win. I told her I would be home after I finished my exam because on Sunday, I will graduate. After I walked across the stage at Rockefeller Chapel, getting my MBA, I immediately handed my diploma to my wife and mother. I will never forget the look on their faces; they were so proud of me. They were crying happy tears. That was one of the highlights of my educational career.

I arrived in Cleveland, met my teammates and coaches, and settled into practicing every day. One of my goals was to go to law school. I made an appointment with the dean of the John Marshall Law School. He informed me that I could not attend law school only during the off-seasons the way I did in business school. I had to attend sequential semesters, during the football season and the off-season; I told him I could do it. I went to football practice with the Cleveland Browns and after practice, I went to John Marshall Law School. I was determined to fulfill my dreams and aspirations of learning how lawyers think. I knew this would prepare me to negotiate contracts in business.

Before I was traded to the Cleveland Browns, the team had won only three games. My first year playing with the Browns, we missed the playoffs by one game. I had the honor and privilege of playing for owner Art Modell, head coaches Forrest Gregg and Sam Rutigliano; and teammates Paul Warfield, Calvin Hill, Greg Coleman, Bill Craven, Ozzie Newsome, Oscar Roan, Greg Pruitt, Mike Pruitt, Mack Mitchell, Tom Darden, Larry Poole, Brian Sipe, Eddie Payton, Clarence Scott, Reggie Rucker, Doug Dieken, Ron Bolton, Earl Edwards, Dick Ambrose, Bob Babich, Charlie Hall, Robert Jackson, Mike St. Clair, Jerry Sherk, Dave Mays, Tom DeLeone, Ricky Feacher, Lyle Alzado, Terry Luck, Cleo Miller, Joe Jones and Don Cockroft, just to name a few. I settled into practice every day, and felt comfortable making a smooth transition to the Cleveland Browns organization and community. We were able to win a lot more games. At the end of the season, it was called "The Turn-Around Year!" The following year, my teammates voted me Defensive Team Captain.

**UNIVERSITY OF CHICAGO MBA,
GRADUATION WITH MYRNA**

GERALD'S CLEVELAND BROWNS PICTURE

When Preparation Meets Opportunity

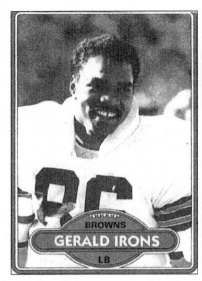

GERALD'S FOOTBALL CARDS

Chapter Twelve

Retiring from the NFL - Service Above Self

When I began my career in the NFL, I told my wife I was going to play ten years and retire. She questioned the number of years, because the average NFL player only played three years. I was confident I would have longevity, because I practiced clean living and a healthy diet, I trained hard, and I had strong faith. After my tenth year of playing, I told the team owner and head coach I was retiring to start Phase Two of my life. I wanted to retire on my own terms. I loved playing in the NFL and have made friends for life; we were a band of brothers.

We moved to Texas, and I began my new career in business. I was able to apply in business everything I learned in college, graduate school and law school; I was like a sponge. Life was good; I had been blessed, and I needed to give back to my community, particularly to the youth. I became an avid community volunteer. My most rewarding endeavor was running for the school board; this was an unpaid volunteer position that defined me in many ways. I made a difference in the lives of parents, teachers and students. I served on the school board for twenty-two years. Right before I retired from the board, the state of Texas awarded our school district Exemplary Rating, the highest distinction for a school district.

We became founding members of our church, Impact Church of The Woodlands. The Woodlands residents voted our family

"Hometown Heroes"; our family had been the first family chosen for this honor.

GERALD ON THE SCHOOL BOARD

When Preparation Meets Opportunity

GERALD AT WORK IN HIS OFFICE

GERALD MEETING WITH PRIME MINISTER OF JAPAN

When Preparation Meets Opportunity

GERALD AND MYRNA AT JAPANESE CONSULATE BALL

Retiring from the NFL - Service Above Self

CISD SCHOOL BOARD

Chapter Thirteen

Prepare Yourself for the Super Bowls of Your Life

Prepare yourself now for the great opportunities in your life. Make a positive difference in your life and in the lives of others. Don't let anyone or any situation define you, unless it enhances you. Do not hang around with negative people; go out of your way to meet impactful people. They are tremendous resources; they are willing to help you reach your destiny. You will get down sometimes, but get up; don't stay down.

Don't give in, give up or quit! When you start something, you must have self-discipline and self-control to finish. You owe it to believe in yourself, and believe you can do all things through Christ. My "Super Bowls" are having parents, in-laws, brothers and sisters who love me; a wife who always encourages me and has my back; three sons who love me and received full scholarships to University of Nebraska, University of Michigan and University of Notre Dame. My youngest son played for the Oakland Raiders and Buffalo Bills. My grandson was named "Student of the Year" and "Unsung Hero". Playing professional football for the Oakland Raiders and Cleveland Browns has been a Super Bowl for me. I live in The Woodlands, Texas with over one hundred thousand people, and I was named one of fifty individuals who influenced our city. I was voted to the Indiana Football Hall of Fame. I am forever grateful for the support and encouragement from the city of my birth, Gary, Indiana; coaches and teachers that helped shape me to be the man that I am today.

GERALD'S FAMILY

Prepare Yourself for the Super Bowls of Your Life

IRONS FAMILY REUNION

MYRNA'S SISTER LESLIE AND NIECE ARIANA

When Preparation Meets Opportunity

MYRNA'S NIECE ALYSSA, BROTHER DEWAYNE AND HER MOTHER

MYRNA'S AND GERALD'S MOTHERS

Prepare Yourself for the Super Bowls of Your Life

CALLOWAY FAMILY (MYRNA'S FAMILY)

MYRNA'S FATHER

When Preparation Meets Opportunity

MYRNA'S MOTHER

Prepare Yourself for the Super Bowls of Your Life

ROMAN, GERALD & MYRNA'S MOTHER

SON GERALD JR.

When Preparation Meets Opportunity

SON JARRETT

SON GRANT

Prepare Yourself for the Super Bowls of Your Life

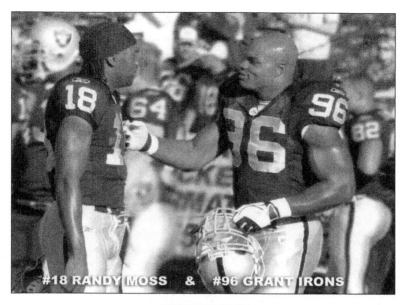

SON GRANT

**INDIANA FOOTBALL HALL OF FAME
INDUCTION BANQUET**

When Preparation Meets Opportunity

THE WOODLANDS HIGH SCHOOL
Commencement
May 1997

GERALD & GRANT AT GRADUATION

Prepare Yourself for the Super Bowls of Your Life

GRANDSON GERALD III

GERALD III

GERALD III

Prepare Yourself for the Super Bowls of Your Life

GERALD, GERALD III AND DR. DON STOCKTON, Superintendent of the Conroe Independent School District

When Preparation Meets Opportunity

IRONS FAMILY

Prepare Yourself for the Super Bowls of Your Life

IRONS FAMILY

**GERALD, GERALD JR., JARRETT,
GRANT & GERALD III**

IRONS FAMILY AT SCHOOL DEDICATION

GERALD WITH MR. AND MRS. AL DAVIS

Prepare Yourself for the Super Bowls of Your Life

GERALD AND COACH JOHN MADDEN

GERALD AND OAKLAND RAIDERS TEAMMATES

When Preparation Meets Opportunity

GERALD AND TEAMMATE CARL WEATHERS

Prepare Yourself for the Super Bowls of Your Life

GERALD AND TEAMMATE CARL WEATHERS

When Preparation Meets Opportunity

TEAMMATE GREG COLEMAN

Prepare Yourself for the Super Bowls of Your Life

MYRNA #86 AND CLEVELAND BROWNS WIVES

GERALD AND MYRNA

When Preparation Meets Opportunity

GERALD AND MYRNA

GERALD, JAMAAL AND JARRETT

Chapter Fourteen

Gerald D. Irons, Sr. Junior High School

I was home one Tuesday evening, feeling very restless. This was my school board meeting night. I had retired from the board, and I missed working with my fellow trustees on behalf of the students.

As I was preparing for bed, I received a telephone call from the school board and superintendent. They informed me that they had voted to name a new school the Gerald D. Irons, Sr. Junior High School. I was stunned and speechless; I felt so honored to have a school named after me. All I could think of was my parents, my wife, sons and grandson who had been on this journey with me. It felt like I just won one hundred Super Bowls. I didn't serve on the school board to get a school named after me. I served on the school board to inspire parents and teachers to encourage their children to work hard and earn a good education. The realization that a school was named after a living person was so moving to me.

This additional legacy was for my two parents, who never went past the eighth-grade and now had a building of higher learning with their name on it. I feel so proud knowing my mother, who is in Heaven, is crying happy tears for me.

GERALD D. IRONS SR. JUNIOR HIGH SCHOOL

GERALD AND MYRNA

GERALD AND MYRNA AT SCHOOL DOOR

Gerald D. Irons, Sr. Junior High School

GERALD AND MYRNA IN FRONT OF SCHOOL

IRONS JUNIOR HIGH SCHOOL

Irons Junior High awarded Students of the Month with a breakfast.

**MYRNA WISE IRONS READING CORNER
IN THE LIBRARY**

Chapter Fifteen
Keys To Success

Success is earned one step at a time; when you get a good education, you are investing in yourself. You are making a big investment in yourself, because what you learn, no one can ever take from you. We all have the power within us to control our destiny.

- Dream big! If no one tells you that your dreams are impossible, then your dreams are not big enough.

- Plan your work and work your plan using self-discipline. Self-discipline is the only discipline that lasts.

- Surround yourself with positive, successful people. Stay away from negative people.

- Look at problems as challenges and opportunities.

- Praise God for all of your victories and successes.

- Do not procrastinate; never put off tomorrow what you can do today.

- Practice being honest and truthful.

- Do not lie, cheat or steal.

- Good character and integrity are non-negotiable.

- Agree to disagree; do not be disagreeable.

- Do not do harm to others.

- Do not become a "couch potato." Learn to eat healthy and exercise regularly. All the success in the world means nothing if you are not healthy enough to enjoy it.

- The wisdom of the future is the past.

- Do what you have to do, until you can do what you want to do.

- Knowledge is power. When knowledge speaks, wisdom listens.

- Value a good education.

- Knowing is not enough. You must put your knowledge into action and application.

- Learning is a life-long journey.

- The decisions you make today will determine your level of success in your future.

- Above all things, never build yourself up at another person's expense.

- Always be a good listener.

- We have two ears, two eyes and only one mouth. We should listen and observe twice as much as we talk.

Keys To Success

- Growth comes through responsibility. Seek it; do not try to avoid it.

- When the team wins, do not worry who will get the credit. There will be enough credit for everyone.

- Treat others the way you want them to treat you.

- We all have the same twenty-four hours in a day; use this time wisely.

- Own your tomorrow.

- You are not a product of your circumstances. You are a product of your decisions.

TRIBUTE TO GERALD

Chapter Sixteen

My Poems

When I was in my language arts class in high school, my teacher would often read poetry to our class. I began to develop a true love for poetry. It was amazing to me how poets could put into words their true feelings of what was happening in their lives, and convert it into beautiful words of wisdom for others to read. One of the poems that touched my young heart, and helped to impact the way I approached life, was a famous poem entitled "The Road Not Taken" by Robert Frost. I especially remembered hearing the end of the poem when my teacher read to our class:

"Two roads diverged in a wood, and I, I took the one less traveled by. And that has made all the difference."

Another person who inspired me to write poetry is my good friend and former teammate, Greg Coleman, retired punter with the Cleveland Browns and Minnesota Vikings. He is a man of honor and integrity.

I have taken the road less traveled by, and it has made all the difference. In times of life's challenges, I have often put into poetic words my expressions of how to deal with them; in an effort to encourage myself to keep striving, keep trusting in God and never giving up on my dreams.

Chapter Seventeen

Poems from a NFL Linebacker

"Being a Rookie"
by
Gerald D. Irons Sr.

Being a rookie is rough, we all know.
But before you're a veteran, it's the path you must go.
So they give you a try-out, on one condition, depending on
How well you can make the transition.

When Preparation Meets Opportunity

Being a rookie is rough, we all know.
You sing and perform in the dining hall each day, knowing
That these are the dues you must pay.

Being a rookie is rough, we all know.
Your college performance was just one requirement, but if you
Aren't good, you will face quick retirement.
The first thing you show is your speed and quickness.
But the first thing you learn is that pro football is a business.

Being a rookie is rough, we all know.
You're playing before millions on national TV; oh, how proud we
Know your family must be. But if you don't hold up under the
Stress and strain, the coach will send you home on an airplane.

Poems from a NFL Linebacker

Being a rookie is rough, we all know.
You save and invest what money you can, while completing your
Degree, should be your master plan.

Being a rookie is rough, we all know.
And when the time comes, when you're old and gray,
To your grandchildren, you will say. . . I was a Dynamite Rookie
In my younger day.

"To Be The BEST"

by

Gerald D. Irons Sr.

To be the BEST is my quest. Athletes come and athletes go,
But there's always something special about a real pro.
See, he's determined to be the very best, and until he is
World Champion. . . he will never rest.

To be the BEST is my quest. I've learned over the years there
Is no shortcut; you've got to work hard at knocking your opponent
On his butt.

To be the BEST is my quest, and execution is the only solution.

While blocking and tackling is my forte...when I finish with

My opponent, he'll need an x-ray.

To be the BEST is my quest. From day to day, towards this goal

I will strive... while keeping my championship hopes alive.

And let's not forget day-to-day concentration, for it will help

Make us the best in the nation.

To be the BEST is my quest. Some may be happy just to make the

Team squad, but I'll never be satisfied 'til I get that

Super Bowl wad. So much happiness I know it will bring, the

Thrill of wearing a Super Bowl Ring.

To be the BEST is my quest. While everything needed I cannot
Mention, I hope the things I've said. . . are not beyond your retention.

"The Trade"

by
Gerald D. Irons Sr.

A trade is made, how much you paid.
Sixpence is a small treasure for such a sweet pleasure.
Oh, how I hope it's fine, this new bottle of wine. . .because
To my ulcer, it must be kind.

A trade is made, how much you paid.
Hundred thousand dollars, which was quite a deal, for a
Shiny new automobile.

A trade is made, how much you paid.
Twenty pesos. . .not bad for a big, strong mule.
At that price, I stole him. . . see, the seller was a fool.

When Preparation Meets Opportunity

A trade is made, how much you paid.
One second-round draft choice. . .oh, he's a big racehorse.
It was such a good deal; everybody knows it was a steal.
He was my first choice; he has the quality of a brand-new
Rolls Royce. Tell us, if you will, just what is his build?
And what are your plans. . .oh, he must stand eighteen hands.
In my assessment, you've made one heck of an investment, cause
After he wins the Triple Crown, for studding duty he is bound.

No! You don't understand, it's not a racehorse. . . it's a MAN.

A trade is made, how much you paid.
Professional football. . .

"What Am I Here For"
by
Gerald D. Irons Sr.

What am I here for, I'd really like to know.
Sometimes I wonder if I should just pack up and go.
When things are going all so wrong, I often wonder
If here is where I belong.

What am I here for, I'd really like to know.
Is it God's will that brings me to this place?
To show and help others avoid disgrace.
I try to help out in every way I can, but it is
Humanly impossible to help every man.

What am I here for, I'd really like to know.
Is it for business opportunities, or for just playing
In the snow? Some people ask, why do you complain; it's not

When Preparation Meets Opportunity

That cold on this terrain. And though they claim it's not
That cold, I'd gladly trade it for a Super Bowl.

So on I go, from day to day, hoping through me others will
Find the right way. And though the grass seems greener on
The other side, I will stay here and do my best because I owe
It to my pride. You see, giving up is just not my cup of tea.
God's grace alone assures eternal life and prosperity.

The fact that I am here, I know it's in God's plan, for He
Loves me more than anyone can. I'll face new challenges
Each and every day, knowing full well that help is on its way.

And if I should doubt tomorrow's outcome, or
ever give up and
California run, just remember. . . for us all
He gave His only begotten Son.

CPSIA information can be obtained at www.ICGtesting.com
Printed in the USA
BVOW06s1025190916

462579BV00010B/29/P